OTHER GIFTBOOKS FOR WOMEN BY HELEN EXLEY:
The Best Of Women's Quotations   Sisters...
Women's Thoughts   Thank heavens for Friends
The Love Between Mothers and Daughters   To a very special Friend

OTHER GIFTBOOKS IN THIS SERIES:
The Glory of Love   Glorious Cats
A Special Collection In Praise Of Mothers   Golf... A Good Walk Spoiled

For Richard.

Published simultaneously in 1996 by Exley Publications
in Great Britain, and Exley Publications LLC in the USA.

12 11 10 9 8 7 6 5 4 3 2 1

Selection and arrangement © Helen Exley 1996
ISBN 1-85015-986-6

Edited and pictures selected by Helen Exley.
Border illustrations by Angela Kerr.
Picture research by Image Select International.
Typeset by Delta, Watford.
Printed in UAE.

Thanks to Margaret Montgomery for her help with text research.

Exley Publications Ltd, 16 Chalk Hill, Watford, Herts WDl 4BN, UK.
Exley Publications LLC, 232 Madison Avenue, Suite 1206, NY 10016, USA.

In
Celebration Of
WOMEN

A SELECTION OF
WORDS AND PAINTINGS
BY
HELEN EXLEY

EXLEY

NEW YORK • WATFORD, UK

1998

In Celebration of
My treasured Friend
Martha on her 40th Bday!
Love,
Diane

*W*omen are the real architects of society.

HARRIET BEECHER STOWE (1811-1896)

We women have always been the ones to construct and

piece together sanctuary and refuge for all our people –

our neighborhoods, our family.

JUNE JORDAN

A woman is the full circle.

Within her is the power to create, nurture,

and transform.

DIANE MARIECHILD

Women never have young minds.

They are born three thousand years old.

SHELAGH DELANEY, b.1939,

FROM *"A TASTE OF HONEY"*

To be a woman is to have interests and duties, raying out in all directions from the central mother-core, like spokes from the hub of a wheel. The pattern of our lives is essentially circular. We must be open to all points of the compass; husband, children, friends, home, community; stretched out, exposed, sensitive like a spider's web to each breeze that blows, to each call that comes. How difficult for us, then, to achieve a balance in the midst of these contradictory tensions, and yet how necessary for the proper functioning of our lives.

ANNE MORROW LINDBERGH, b.1906,
FROM *"GIFT FROM THE SEA"*

$\mathcal{A}$s women we must learn to become leaders in society, not just for our own sake, but for the sake of all people. We must support and protect our kinship with the environment for the generations to come.

C. GALLAND

If a woman can only succeed by emulating men, I think it is
a great loss and not a success. The aim is not only for a woman to succeed,
but to keep her womanhood and let her womanhood influence society.

SUZANNE BROGGER, b.1944, FROM *"WOMEN"* BY NAIM ATTALLAH

As you know, certain studies show that women traditionally lead by means of reconciliation, interrelations and persuasion, considering the fact that society has traditionally counted on the women to keep the family together, while men usually lead through control and intimidation.

When women entered the fields of politics and business, they brought with them the moral values they had learned from home. These values have shown good results; I dare say they have even shown better results than did the traditional model created by men.... There are several ways in which men do not understand women. There is evidence of this everywhere. I think it is time that male leaders look to women leaders as role models. They will find that persuasion brings better results than confrontation. And, finally, they will realize that, when dealing with the nations of the world, reconciliation unites people and allows them to work together for the benefit of all.

VIOLETA CHAMORRO,
FROM INTRODUCTION SPEECH FOR INTERNATIONAL HALL OF FAME

"I AM STRONG. I'M INVINCIBLE. I AM WOMAN."

So says the pop song, and so say women down through the centuries, as
they affirm their status alongside men in this world. They may not have
fought in a war, but they have fought many other, equally tortuous
battles. And sometimes they have won. Sometimes they have lost. But
they remain undefeated.... The loving, giving and gaining, the hurts,
hang-ups and hormones, the breath-taking dexterity with which we juggle
countless different jobs and play many different parts, and the exhaustion
it causes, are all integral parts of women's pilgrimage.

MICHELE GUINNESS,
FROM "TAPESTRY OF VOICES"

In a society where the rights and potential of women are constrained, no man can be truly free. He may have power, but he will not have freedom.

MARY ROBINSON, PRESIDENT OF IRELAND

One of the wonderful things about women, which I don't think

many social anthropologists have fully understood, is that we are

bonded by shared experiences – by babies and the rituals and

problems of our bodies. Men need gambits to open conversations

with other men. Women don't, because a sense of camaraderie and

mutual interest already exists between us.

ANITA RODDICK, b.1943, FROM *"BODY AND SOUL"*

Doing it for ourselves is the essence of the women's movement: it keeps us honest, keeps us real, keeps us concrete. And it is that doing *– not just being, feeling, or sweeping the floor that gets dirty again – which brings women into history. It is* new *for women to be making history – not just a few queens, empresses or exceptional geniuses, but hundreds, thousands, millions of women now entering history, knowing we have made history – by changing our own lives. The most superficial view of the daily paper – front page, sports page, financial page, want ads – shows not only the entrance of women into the actions and professions from which they were barred (the Little League, the police and fire departments, submarines, governor, mayor, Episcopal priest, Conservative rabbi, radical terrorist, orchestra conductor, Wall Street broker), but the transformation of the political, economic, theological and cultural agenda (the very language, the style, the questions addressed) and also the transformation of the women's page: lifestyle, of importance to men.*

BETTY FRIEDAN, b.1921, FROM *"IT CHANGED MY LIFE"*

Women never have an half-hour in all their lives (excepting before or after anybody is up in the house) that they can call their own, without fear of offending or of hurting someone. Why do people sit up so late, or, more rarely, get up so early? Not because the day is not long enough, but because they have "no time in the day to themselves."

FLORENCE NIGHTINGALE (1820-1910), FROM *"CASSANDRA"*

Women must be still as the axis of a wheel in the midst of her activities... she must be the pioneer in achieving this stillness, not only for her own salvation, but for the salvation of family life, of society, perhaps even of our civilization.

ANNE MORROW LINDBERGH, b.1906, FROM *"GIFT FROM THE SEA"*

On the day when it will be possible for woman to love not in her weakness but in her strength, not to escape herself but to find herself, not to abase herself but to assert herself – on that day love will become for her, as for man, a source of life and not of mortal danger.

SIMONE DE BEAUVOIR (1908-1986)

Who knows what women can be when they are finally free to become themselves? Who knows what women's intelligence will contribute when it can be nourished without denying love? Who knows of the possibilities of love when men and women share not only children, home, and garden, not only the fulfillment of their biological roles, but the responsibilities and passions of the work that creates the human future. It has barely begun, the search of women for themselves.

BETTY FRIEDAN, b. 1921, FROM *"THE FEMININE MYSTIQUE"*

Being nice should *never* be perceived as being weak. It's not a sign of weakness, it's a sign of courtesy, manners, grace, a woman's ability to make everyone... feel at home, and it should never be construed as weakness.... Men are comfortable with being intimidating; a woman is not comfortable with the thought that she is intimidating, and therefore, perhaps she tries to be a little informal, but that doesn't mean that the woman can't be tough when the time arises....

BENAZIR BHUTTO, b.1953,
PRIME MINISTER OF PAKISTAN

The Hidden Sun

Originally, woman was the sun.
She was an authentic person.
But now woman is the moon.
She lives by depending on another
and she shines by reflecting
another's light.
Her face has a sickly pallor.

We must now regain our hidden sun.
"Reveal our hidden sun!
Rediscover our natural gifts!"
This is the ceaseless cry
Which forces itself into our hearts;
It is our final,
complete,
and only instinct
through which
our various
separate instincts
are unified.

HIRATSUKA RAICHO

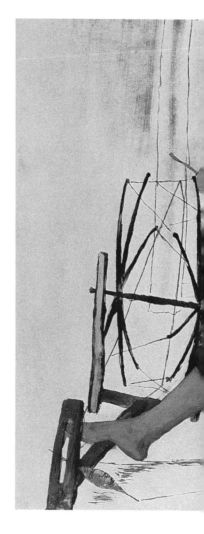

... none of us is Superwoman.

We are by turns industrious woman, harried

woman, organized woman and sometimes

cunning woman, because we all agree that

one can always find time, in the

most hard-pressed life, to do what one really

wants to do, whether it is dancing the

tango, playing the harp or writing a book.

VALERIE GROVE,
FROM *"THE COMPLEAT WOMAN"*

Y ou have tampered with women,
you have struck a rock.

SOUTH AFRICAN WOMEN'S PROTEST SLOGAN, 1957

... I'm not going to lie down and let
trouble walk over me.

ELLEN GLASGOW (1874-1945)

I am deliberate
and afraid
of nothing.

AUDRE LORDE, b.1934, FROM *"NEW YEAR'S DAY"*

A mother who dedicates her life, body and soul, to her husband and her family is loved and cherished – and despised. Though the word would never enter their minds.

Thousands of years have brainwashed men into believing women are in the world to take care of them. Anything else is treason and unwomanly.

A nun who has lived a full, adventurous, intellectual life is considered to have wasted her existence. An unmarried woman must be a trifle odd.

For the sake of the sons – and even for the sons' future wives – a woman must keep a part of her mind and heart entirely for herself. Every family is better off with a wife and mother who can astonish and occasionally bewilder.

PAM BROWN, b.1928

There has never been any question but that women of the poor should toil alongside their men. No angry, and no compassionate, voice has been raised to say that women should not break their backs with harvest work, or soil their hands with blacking grates and peeling potatoes. The objection is only to work that is pleasant, exciting or profitable – the work that any human being might think it worthwhile to do.

DOROTHY L. SAYERS (1893-1957),
FROM *"UNPOPULAR OPINIONS"*

At dawn, when the sun is just a sliver of pink, and acacia trees with grotesque silhouettes scratch at the sky, a round of cocks crowing – one from the seat of a tractor, one from an overturned oil can, one from the thatched roof of the granary – wakens women in the drylands of Africa. As one body they rise, tie their scarves round their heads and their babies on their backs, set sticks to burn under cooking pots, slop food for chickens and pigs, pile porridge in bowls, curse the dog, queue for the standpipe. As the sun rises – a malevolent orange eye – they step onto the track, worn through the bush by generations of work-hardened feet, and make their way to the land for the day.

Dawn in Asia's wet plains sets women stirring too: crawling from their folds of mosquito net, wrapping their saris tight, blowing life into charcoals, coaxing children to eat rice, and calves to eat gruel, driving buffalo to the mist-shrouded paddy fields, then stepping into tepid brown water and bending as they will bend all day.

A church bell ringing and dogs barking nudge Andean women awake. A prayer is whispered, a skirt fastened, water hauled from the well in the village square, goats tethered and milked into an old aluminium bucket, beans heated and tipped onto tin plates. Then, closing a rickety door, they step onto the steep, stony track that winds down from their houses to the fields.

Others are woken by prayer calls from mosque minarets; by donkeys braying under olive trees; by cows lowing, their udders swollen and tender with milk. These women, who live in the world's rural areas, are farmers in everything but name. And their labor produces half of the world's food.

DEBBIE TAYLOR, FROM "WOMEN: AN ANALYSIS" IN *"WOMEN: A WORLD REPORT"*

My great hope is that at this marvelous

moment for women, they should remember that

one of the gifts they have is that they remained

so very close to the personal life, and that the

qualities that were discovered in the personal

life, the value of human life, the value of

tenderness, the attentiveness to others' moods,

the need for compassion and pity and

understanding, the things that women practice

every day in their daily lives, in their small

kingdoms, are enormously important.

ANAÏS NIN (1903-1977), FROM "A WOMAN SPEAKS"

No one sex can govern alone. I believe that one of the reasons why civilization has failed so lamentably is that it has had one-sided government.

NANCY ASTOR (1879-1964), FROM *"MY TWO COUNTRIES"*

'Tis woman's strongest vindication for speaking that
the world needs to hear her voice.
It would be subversive of every human interest that
the cry of one-half the human family be stifled....
The world has had to limp along with
the wobbling gait and one-sided hesitancy of a man
with one eye. Suddenly the bandage is
removed from the other eye and the whole body is
filled with light. It sees a circle where
before it saw a segment. The darkened eye restored,
every member rejoices with it.

ANNA JULIA COOPER

… there are two ways of going about liberation: one, of course, is the political way, changing the laws and fighting for equalities. There are so many ways of doing it. But the other I stress simply because it is the one I know: the psychological way, which is the removal of obstacles so that you can create your own freedom and you don't have to ask for it. You don't have to wait for it to be given to you. And the women I chose as my heroines were women who created their own freedom. They didn't demand it, they didn't ask for it. They created it. Something in themselves made them independent women, and this kind of independence I stress. Because the other feeling that has been taught women really is the blaming of society or the blaming of men for the situation in which we find ourselves. Now I found through psychology that when I put the blame on others I felt I was practically saying: "I am a helpless, passive victim." And it's a depressing thought! So the day I saw beyond that, at a certain moment in psychology, I saw: "No, not at all. I am the master of my destiny." When I feel free and independent and behave in a certain way towards a relationship, that affects the relationship. I can have an effect on it; I can have an effect on the person I am working for, on my publisher. It is very easy to blame society or to blame the man, but it actually makes you feel even more helpless. Because that means that you are waiting for the man to liberate you, for the government to liberate you or for history. And that takes a long time. It takes centuries, and it's too slow for me.
We have only one life.

ANAÎS NIN (1903-1977), FROM *"A WOMAN SPEAKS"*

The here, the now, and the individual, have always been the special concern of the saint, the artist, the poet, and – from time immemorial – the woman. In the small circle of the home she has never quite forgotten the particular uniqueness of each member of the family; the spontaneity of now; the vividness of here. This is the basic substance of life. These are the individual elements that form the bigger entities like mass, future, world. We may neglect these elements, but we cannot dispense with them. They are the drops that make up the stream. They are the essence of life itself. It may be our special function to emphasize again these neglected realities, not as a retreat from greater responsibilities but as a first real step toward a deeper understanding and solution of them. When we start at the center of ourselves, we discover something worthwhile extending toward the periphery of the circle. We find again some of the joy in the now, some of the peace in the here, some of the love in me and thee which go to make up the kingdom of heaven on earth.

ANNE MORROW LINDBERGH, b.1906, FROM *"GIFT FROM THE SEA"*

*W*omen... think that perhaps whatever they achieve is at the expense of their personal world and will somehow destroy their personal world. They never thought that whatever they became was in turn poured back into the personal world and enriched it, that they were enriching their children, they were enriching their husband, they were enriching their neighbors. We stopped really believing that the enrichment of the individual is actually what enriches our collective life. We forgot that. And for woman it was worse because she was not expected to produce in the first place. She was not expected to create. Culture didn't demand it of her; it didn't demand of her to become the best doctor or the best lawyer or the best painter or the best writer; it didn't demand anything of her except the fulfillment of her personal duties. So this was not an incentive for woman to develop whatever gift she had.

ANAÎS NIN (1903-1977), FROM *"A WOMAN SPEAKS"*

Woman must not accept; she must challenge. She must not be awed by that which has been built up around her; she must reverence that woman in her which struggles for expression.

MARGARET H. SANGER (1879-1966)

I don't wish women to have power over men – but over themselves.

SIMONE DE BEAUVOIR (1908-1986)

A slave is still a slave if she refuses to think for herself.

IBO PROVERB

One of the things about equality is not just that you be treated equally to a man, but that you treat yourself equally to the way you treat a man.

MARLO THOMAS, b.1943

Women have belly and they would stand up, and all you man only study to go inside the rum shop. All you who want to go, go, cause all you dis is worms feedin on de union. We suffer so long here and we must sacrifice, and if we have to eat dirt we must eat it, and if we have to eat brick we must eat it, before we go back to that condition we was in, and if we have to eat grass we will eat grass.

SAHEEDAN RAMROOP, b.1922,
(CANE-CUTTER)

A MOTHER IS A PERSON

a mother is a person
who gives birth
cleans up messes
kisses dirty faces
makes thousands of peanut butter sandwiches
and says no more often than yes

a mother is a person
who acts as chauffeur
personal secretary
and general contractor
housebreaks and feeds the dog
hunts for numerous articles
and hurts when her child is hurt

a mother is a person
who needs to remember
she is a person

MARY ELEANORE RICE, FROM *"IMAGES: WOMEN IN TRANSITION"*

WOMEN LEADERS – A STYLE OF THEIR OWN

The talent of women for communion, nurturing, and intuitive action has never been more needed than now, as we strive to meet the diverse cultural and environmental challenges of our times. Patriarchy, hierarchy, and obedience to a higher authority all have run their historical course. Governments, families, and businesses built on these unyielding principles of organization are toppling, giving way to more elastic feminine forms of cooperation, communication, and wholeness.

CAROL SPENARD LA RUSSO

Men have the grand vision, and they pass it on to somebody else to put into practice. Women follow the details more, they want to know that it *is* being put into practice.

MARY EUGENIA CHARLES, PRIME MINISTER, COMMONWEALTH OF DOMINICA

Males use a hard style of leadership that stresses hierarchy, dominance and order. Women, on the other hand, exercise leadership characterized by a soft style of cooperation, influence and empowerment.

MICHAEL A. GENOVESE, FROM *"WOMEN AS NATIONAL LEADERS"*

What has counted for women historically is to organize, organize, and then organize some more.

LAURA LISWOOD, FROM *"WOMEN WORLD LEADERS"*

Woman must come of age by herself. This is the essence of "coming of age" – to learn how to stand alone. She must learn not to depend on another, nor to feel she must prove her strength by competing with another. In the past, she has swung between these two opposite poles of dependence and competition, of Victorianism and Feminism. Both extremes throw her off balance; neither is the center, the true center of being a whole woman. She must find her true center alone. She must become whole. She must, it seems to me, as a prelude to any "two solitudes" relationship, follow the advice of the poet to become "world to oneself for another's sake."

ANNE MORROW LINDBERGH, b.1906, FROM *"GIFT FROM THE SEA"*

Remember always that you have not only the right to be an individual; you have an obligation to be one. *You cannot make any useful contribution in life unless you do this.*

ELEANOR ROOSEVELT (1884-1962), FROM *"YOU LEARN BY LIVING"*

The men who are brought up to respect women, the men who are brought up to respect the earth as woman, think of the earth and the woman as one and the same, are the real men.

Everything that gives birth is female. When men begin to understand the relationships of the universe that women have always known, the world will begin to change for the better.

Teachings come from the women, all the teachings. All the teachings come from the woman. The devastation of all these governments and all these countries is because they put women down. Put the women down, your place is not going to work.

When you honor women it's going to work.

CECILIA MITCHELL (A MOHAWK), FROM STEVE WELL *"WISDOM'S DAUGHTERS"*

The mother is the most precious possession of the nation, so precious that society advances its highest well-being when it protects the functions of the mother.

ELLEN KEY (1849-1926)

To nourish children and raise them against odds is in any time, any place, more valuable than to fix bolts in cars or design nuclear weapons.

MARILYN FRENCH, b.1929

Now as ever men rage and wander, come and go as they sometimes must, but woman out of her natural link with the way of the earth and with her body in the service of small children will incline to stay. Staying is the start of all civility.

MICHAEL ADAMS, FROM "WOMENKIND: A CELEBRATION"

Women understand the problems of the nation better than men for women have solved the problems of human life from embryo to birth and from birth to maturity. Women are the survival kit of the human race.

COUNCILLOR MANDIZVIDZA OF MUCHEKE TOWNSHIP, ZIMBABWE, 1983

It seems a contradiction and denial of their sex that women should
risk the very thing which only they can nurture and sustain,
namely life itself. Yet despite being hemmed in by society's barriers,
their vision obscured by fixed horizons, their growth stunted and their
potential to develop forced into the narrow channels
leading to marriage and motherhood, women throughout the centuries
have managed to transcend their condition and reach out for the world.
The reason is clear. If they are to do more
than simply give life – if they are to enrich it as well – then the journey
must be made which takes them beyond the physical and mental
confines set by society. That women are capable of grasping
this aspect of their destiny has been ably demonstrated by those
pioneers who, valuing freedom more than conformity, have walked out
into the world and taken possession of it.

MARY RUSSELL, FROM *"THE BLESSINGS OF A GOOD THICK SKIRT"*

Setbacks that discourage can be viewed as fresh opportunities to speak up and continue to address not only women's issues, but fundamental human issues. We can welcome these challenges as new platforms for change. Freedom is not easily won, and must be fought for courageously daily, as any member of an underclass will testify.

CAROL SPENARD LA RUSSO

If you think you're too small to have an impact, try going to bed with a mosquito.

ANITA RODDICK

**... as one goes through life one
learns that if you don't paddle
your own canoe, you don't move.**

KATHARINE HEPBURN, b.1909

I think the very restrictions which were put on woman which made her emphasize the personal world caused something very good to be born. Whereas men dealt in terms of nations, in terms of statistics, abstract ideology, woman, because her world was restricted to the personal, was more human. Now that she is beginning to step beyond her confines, I hope she can bring to the world the sense of the personal value of human beings, some empathy and some sympathy.

ANAÏS NIN (1903-1977),
FROM *"A WOMAN SPEAKS"*

WOMEN TOGETHER! FOR A NEW WORLD

You and I will fold the sheets
Advancing towards each other
From Burma, from Lapland,

From India where the sheets have been washed in the river
And pounded upon stones:
Together we will match the corners.

From China where women on either side of the river
Have washed their pale cloth in the White Stone Shallows
"Under the shining moon".

We meet as though in the formal steps of a dance
To fold the sheets together, put them to air
In wind, in sun over bushes, or by the fire.

We stretch and pull from one side and then the other –
Your turn. Now mine.
We fold them and put them away until they are needed.

A wish for all people when they lie down to sleep –
Smooth linen, cool cotton, the fragrance and stir of herbs
And the faint but perceptible scent of sweet clear water.

ROSEMARY DOBSON, FROM "THE THREE FATES"

I struggle to live for the beauty of a pansy

for a little black baby's song

for my lover's laugh

I struggle for the blaze of pink

across the evening sky

for some bar-b-cue ribs

I struggle for life and the pursuit of its happiness

I struggle to fill my house with joy

STEPHANIE BYRD, FROM "EVERY DAY"

I call up my names: Woman who has been born in the arms of a woman and welcomed home. I shout truth teller, silence breaker, life embracer, death no longer fearing, woman reunited with her child self. I sing woman who is daughter, sister, lover and mother to herself. I hum woman planter, gatherer, healer. I drum woman warrior, siren, woman who stands firmly on her feet, woman who reaches inward to her center and outward to stars. I am woman who is child no longer, woman who is making herself sane, whole.

ANDREA R. CANAAN

IT IS TIME

From Steve Well's *"Wisdom's Daughters"*

It is time for the woman. It is time to talk and set things right,
for women to stand up. And when the world honors women, the mothers, and
Mother Earth, everyone will be better off.

CECILIA MITCHELL (A MOHAWK)

Women have to be recognized. The words of women have to be recognized.
The women will come out. It might be prophesied or doesn't
have to be prophesied, but the feeling is so strong that the women will come
out and voice their feelings. Whether people want to
hear it or not, it's going to come because it's meant to be. It's that time.

VICKIE DOWNEY (A PUEBLO)

This is the time of women, and there's a new movement across the country.
Women are getting up on their hind legs. Women have to rise in the nation and
internationally. We have to be more involved in politics and decision making.

BETTY LAVERDURE (AN OJIBWAY)

It is vain to say human beings ought to be satisfied with tranquillity: they must have action; and they will make it if they cannot find it. Millions are condemned to a stiller doom than mine, and millions are in silent revolt against their lot. Nobody knows how many rebellions besides political rebellions ferment in the masses of life which people earth. Women are supposed to be very calm generally. But women feel just as men feel: they need exercise for their faculties, and a field for their efforts, as much as their brothers do; they suffer from too rigid a restraint, too absolute a stagnation, precisely as men would suffer; and it is narrow-minded in their more privileged fellow-creatures to say that they ought to confine themselves to making puddings and knitting stockings, to playing on the piano and embroidering bags. It is thoughtless to condemn them, or laugh at them, if they seek to do more or learn more than custom has pronounced necessary for their sex.

CHARLOTTE BRONTË (1816-1855), FROM *"JANE EYRE"*

If it wasn't for the women, women
We would not be living, living
We would not be joyful, singing
Loving and beloved women

If it wasn't for the women
What would we do?
We wouldn't have
Health or strength or beauty
We wouldn't have a home
And we wouldn't have food
If it wasn't for the work
Of the women.

If it wasn't for the women
What would we do?
We wouldn't have
Art or craft or music
We wouldn't have love
And we wouldn't have truth
If it wasn't for the work
Of the women

ALIX DOBKIN

At my age I care to my roots about the quality of women, and I care because I know how important her quality is. The hurt that women have borne so long may have immeasurable meaning. We women are the meeting place of the highest and the lowest, and of minutiae and riches; it is for us to see, and understand, and have pride in representing ourselves truly. Perhaps we must say to man… "The time may have come for us to forge our own identity, dangerous as that will be."

FLORIDA SCOTT-MAXWELL

You are the architect of your personal experience.

SHIRLEY MACLAINE, b.1934

Women are always being tested... but ultimately, each of us has to define who we are individually and then do the very best job we can to grow into that.

HILLARY RODHAM CLINTON

If you give in to intimidation, you'll go on being intimidated.

AUNG SAN SUU KYI

Be critical. Women have the right to say: "This is surface, this falsifies reality, this degrades".

TILLIE OLSEN

Nobody can make you feel inferior without your consent.

ELEANOR ROOSEVELT (1884-1962)

We reject pedestals, queenhood, and walking ten paces behind.
To be recognized as human, levelly human, is enough.

COMBAHEE RIVER COLLECTIVE

To me equality is the important thing. I don't want preferences,
I don't want to be preferred as a woman. But I want
it acknowledged that I am a human being who has the capacity to do
what I have to do, and it doesn't matter whether I was born
a man or woman. The work will be done that way.

MARY EUGENIA CHARLES, PRIME MINISTER,
COMMONWEALTH OF DOMINICA

*T*he world cannot do without women...
the future lies with us.

JOAN COLLINS, b.1933

I hear the singing of the lives of women,
The clear mystery, the offering and pride.

MURIEL RUKEYSER (1913-1980)

Each woman is far from average in the daily heroics
of her life, even though she may never receive a
moment's recognition in history.

INTRODUCTION TO *"WOMEN & WORK"*, NEWSAGE PRESS

Women once knew their place – and so do we.
Our home is the universe. Our task is anything
we set our minds and hearts to.

MAYA V. PATEL, b.1943

PICTURE CREDITS

Cover: **The Virgins,** *Gustav Klimt*, National Gallery, Prague
Archiv für Kunst.

Title page: **Vahine no te Vi,** *Paul Gauguin*, Baltimore, Museum of Art, Archiv für Kunst.

page 6: © 1996 *W. Russell Flint*, Chris Beetles Gallery.

page 8: **The Reader,** *Henri Fantin-Latour*, Musée D'Orsay, Art Resource.

pages 10/11: **Per 80 centesimi,** *A. Morbelli*, Vercelli, Museo Civico Borgogna, Archivi Alinari, Florence.

page 13: **Lady Palmer,** © 1996 *Sir Frank Dicksee*, Roy Miles Gallery, The Bridgeman Art Library.

pages 14/15: © 1996 *Peter Fiore*, Artworks, New York.

page 16: **Stacking the hay,** *Vincent Van Gogh*, Edimedia.

page 18: **Washerwomen,** *Marie Petiet*, Musée Petiet, Edimedia.

page 21: **Antonia,** © 1996 *Thomas Durkin*, Bonhams, London, The Bridgeman Art Library.

page 22: **Parisian Woman,** *Pierre Auguste Renoir*, Statens Konstmuseer, Stockholm.

page 24: **Lady Fishing, Mrs. Ormond, 1889,** *John Singer Sargent*, Tate Gallery, London, Art Resource, New York.

page 27: **The Spanish Girl,** © 1996 *Gerald Kelly*, Atkinson Art Gallery, The Bridgeman Art Library.

pages 28/9: **The Black Brook,** *John Singer Sargent*, Tate Gallery, London, Art Resource, New York.

pages 30/31: **Whilst Spinning and Weaving,** © 1996 *Nguyen Duc Nung*, Archiv für Kunst.

page 32: **Two Dancers,** *Edgar Degas*, Private Collection, Edimedia.

page 35: **Anna Washington Derry,** © 1996 *Laura Wheeler Waring*, National Museum of American Art, Smithsonian Institution, Gift of the Harmon Foundation, Art Resource.

pages 36/7: **The Hay Harvest,** © 1996 *Boris Kustodiev*, Scala.

pages 38/9: **Picking Potatoes,** © 1996 *Richard Birnstengel*, City Art Collection, Chemnitz, Archiv für Kunst.

page 40: **In risaia,** *Angelo Morbelli*, Boston Museum of Fine Arts, Archivi Alinari, Florence.

page 43: **After the Bath,** *Joaquin y Bastida Sorolla*, Museo Sorolla, Madrid, The Bridgeman Art Library.

page 44: **Women,** © 1996 *Izzat Klychev*, Tret'jakov Gallery, Moscow, Edimedia.

page 47: **Thoughts of the Past,** *J.R. Spencer Stanhope*, Tate Gallery, London, Art Resource, New York.

page 49: **Before Bedtime,** © 1996 *Robert Gemmell Hutchinson*, Private Collection, The Bridgeman Art Library.

pages 50/51: **Nel negozio di cappelli,** *Edgar Degas*, Art Institute of Chicago, Scala.

page 53: **Fransk Bondgumma,** © 1996 *Jenny Nyström-Stoopendal*, Statens Konstmuseer, Stockholm.

page 54: **Head of a Jamaican Girl,** © 1996 *Augustus John*, Private Collection, The Bridgeman Art Library.

page 57: **Mother and Child,** © 1996 *Mary Cassatt*, Private Collection, Giraudon / Art Resource.

page 59: **Portrait of Madame Redon sewing,** *Odilon Redon*, Art Resource.

page 61: **The Milliner,** *Henri de Toulouse-Lautrec*, Musée Toulouse-Lautrec, Albi, France, Art Resource.

page 63: **Woman in a tulip field,** © 1996 *George Hitchcock*, Archiv für Kunst.

page 64: **The Apple of Her Eye,** *Robert McGregor*, Fine Art Photographic Library.

page 67: **Portrait of a girl,** © 1996 *Michail Nesterov*, Scala.

page 69: *Vassili Sourikov*, Tret'jakov Gallery, Moscow.

page 71: **La Coiffure,** *Edgar Degas*, Private Collection, Edimedia.

pages 72/3: **Beim Knüpfen der Seile für die Wasserschaufel,** © 1996 *Tran Van Can*, Archiv für Kunst.

page 75: **A Portrait of the Artist's Wife Sewing at a Table,** *Peder Severin Kroyer*, Fine Art Photographic Library.

page 76: **Model Resting,** © 1996 *Cogghe*, Giraudon.

page 79: **Portrait of Mother,** © 1996 *Bruno Cassinari*, Raccolta Della Ragione, Firenze, Art Resource.

page 80: **Girls on the Heights,** © 1996 *Charles Curran*, Private Collection, The Bridgeman Art Library.

page 83: **The Beethoven Frieze,** *Gustav Klimt*, Austrian Gallery, Vienna, Art Resource.

page 84: **Portrait of Frau M.B.,** © 1996 *Franz Tippel*, Dresden, Gemäldegalerie, Neue Meister, Archiv für Kunst.

page 87: © 1996 *P. Kotov*, Edimedia.

pages 88/9: **Shadow and Sunlight,** © 1996 *Allan Rohan Crite*, National Museum of American Art, Smithsonian Institute, The Bridgeman Art Library.

page 91: **Testa,** *D. Guerello*, Private Collection, Archivi Alinari, Florence.

TEXT CREDITS